Massachusetts Real Estate Broker Exam

"You never fail until you stop trying" - Albert Einstein

For inquiries;
info@xmprep.com

Massachusetts Real Estate Broker Exam #1

Test Taking Tips

☐ Take a deep breath and relax

☐ Read directions carefully

☐ Read the questions thoroughly

☐ Make sure you understand what is being asked

☐ Go over all of the choices before you answer

☐ Paraphrase the question

☐ Eliminate the options you know are wrong

☐ Check your work

☐ Think positively and do your best

Table of Contents

TEST DIRECTION

DIRECTIONS

Read the questions carefully and then choose the ONE best answer to each question.

Be sure to allocate your time carefully so you are able to complete the entire test within the testing session. You may go back and review your answers at any time.

You may use any available space in your test booklet for scratch work.

Questions in this booklet are not actual test questions but they are the samples for commonly asked questions.

This test aims to cover all topics which may appear on the actual test. However some topics may not be covered.

Studying this booklet will be preparing you for the actual test. It will not guarantee improving your test score but it will help you pass your exam on the first attempt.

Some useful tips for answering multiple choice questions;

- Start with the questions that you can easily answer.

- Underline the keywords in the question.

- Be sure to read all the choices given.

- Watch for keywords such as NOT, always, only, all, never, completely.

- Do not forget to answer every question.

CONTINUE ▶

1

In an assignment, which of the following is the responsibility of the original tenant?

A) The assignee
B) The landlord
C) The managing agent
D) None of the above

2

A **percolation test** refers to a test that determines the water absorption rate of soil in preparation for the building of a septic drain field or infiltration basin.

Which of the following administers percolation test?

A) Department of Buildings
B) Department of Health
C) Tax assessor
D) Building inspector

3

Homeowner's insurance refers to a type of property insurance which covers losses and damages to an individual's house and assets in the home.

Which of the following does not cover by standard coverage homeowner policy?

A) Flood
B) Fire
C) Theft
D) Vandalism

4

Which of the following results from the death of the landlord?

A) Automatic renewal of the lease
B) An indefinite extension of the lease
C) Termination of the lease
D) Cheers and cartwheels

5

Which of the following losses does liability insurance protect the insured?

A) Falls by delivery persons
B) Fire
C) Windstorm
D) All of the above

6

Which of the following given items below is not a necessary element of a contract?

A) Meeting of the minds
B) Earnest money
C) Competent parties
D) Consideration

7

Lien refers to the official order allowing someone to keep a person's property who owes them money until there is full payment.

Which of the following determines the priority of a lien?

A) Date of the court hearing
B) Date of making the lien
C) Date of paying off the lien
D) Date of recording the lien

8

All building tenants use meeting spaces, lobbies, restrooms and other amenities in which landlords also charge for the use of these spaces.

Which of the following is the basis of an office-building tenant in paying rent?

A) Viable square feet
B) Usable square feet
C) Carpetable square feet
D) Rentable square feet

9

Which of the following does a mortgage broker need to disclose to a loan applicant?

A) The number of lenders that will be solicited by the broker
B) Application fees
C) Conditions for fee refunds
D) All of the above

10

Which of the following refers to an executed contract?

A) Not yet fully signed
B) Fully signed
C) Not yet fully completed
D) Fully completed

11

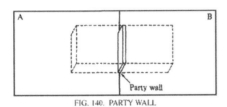

FIG. 140. PARTY WALL

Which of the following does a party wall become an example as shown in the above image?

A) Appurtenance
B) Easement
C) Encroachment
D) Incoherent

12

Which of the following personnel must a broker subordinate his or her personal interests?

A) Client
B) Customer
C) Sales agent
D) Third party

13

Special assessment designates a unique charge in which government units can assess against real estate parcels for specific public projects.

Which of the following pays special assessment?

A) Only those property owners that will experience a benefit from the assessment
B) All property owners in the community
C) All residents of the community
D) None of the above

14

Real estate appraisal describes the process of creating an opinion of value for real property.

Which of the following is determined in a property first by a tax assessor like a real estate appraiser?

A) Mortgage value
B) Market Value
C) Insured value
D) Assessed value

15

A **capital improvement** refers to the addition of a permanent structural change or the restoration of a property that will either enhance the property's overall value, increases its useful life or adapts it to a new use.

Which of the following costs is considered to be a capital improvement rather than an expense?

A) Roof replacement
B) Brokerage commission
C) A for-sale sign on the property
D) Addition of a two-car garage

16

Which of the following refers to the document whereby a purchaser of property personally obligates him or herself to the lender?

A) Bond
B) Deed
C) Mortgage
D) Power of Attorney

17

An **asset base** is the underlying assets that give value to a company, investment or loan.

Which of the following refers to a basis whereby an asset is depreciated at the same amount in each accounting period?

A) Short-term basis
B) Deductible basis
C) Straight line basis
D) None of the above

18

Which of the following organizations may impose liability for clean up of real estate contaminated by toxic substances?

A) NHPA
B) NEPA
C) CERCLA
D) None of the answers are correct.

19

Which of the following is called for redemption occurs after a foreclosure sale and a redemption that happens before, respectively?

A) Equitable, statutory
B) Statutory, equitable
C) Judicial, nonjudicial
D) Civil, equitable

20

Which of the following scenario will the state mandated disclosure statement be presented to prospective customers or clients?

A) At the first substantive meeting
B) When there is a meeting of the minds
C) When the transaction goes into contract
D) Only if the customer or client buys or sells a property through the broker

21

Usury became common first in England under the rule of King Henry VIII.

Which of the following most accurately describes usury?

A) An illegal use of another's property
B) Charging fees for borrowing money
C) Charging an illegally high interest rate for borrowed funds
D) Commonplace, ordinary

22

Which of the following happens for a taxpayer with passive losses but exceeds the allowable limit for that year?

A) The allowable limit goes up the same amount the following year.

B) The loss may be carried over to a future year when the taxpayer meets passive activity limit loss rules.

C) The lost passive is gone which can only be used in the specified tax year.

D) The taxpayer will be penalized about 10% for the over the limit amount.

23

In investing, the **cash-on-cash return** refers to the ratio of annual before-tax cash flow to the total cash invested amount in percentage that is widely used to evaluate the cash flow from income-producing assets.

Which of the following is the cash on cash return of an investment having a $90,000 cash flow and a cash investment of $500,000?

A) 17%

B) 18%

C) 19%

D) 20%

24

"Jurisdiction in rem" describes the exercise of power by a court over property or a "status" against a person over whom the court does not have "in personam jurisdiction."

Which of the following is against in an in-rem procedure?

A) Retail business owner

B) Property owner

C) Property

D) Municipal government

25

Married couples registers as business partners, and decides to list their house for sale.

The Husband met with Real Estate Representative and told him that he and his wife would give her the listing. Husband signed the listing agreement.

The representative had no idea that the Wife was not an owner of the property.

Which of the following is the status of the listing agreement?

A) Void

B) Valid

C) Voidable

D) Unenforceable

26

A **quitclaim deed** refers to an instrument used in transferring interest in real property.

Which of the following is the use of quitclaim deed?

A) Transfer property from an estate to an heir.
B) Foreclose on a property by a lender.
C) Restore mining rights.
D) Remove a cloud on the title.

27

Easements are rights given to a person or entity to trespass upon or use land owned by somebody else. Landlocked homeowners sometimes pay for an easement to cross the land of another to reach their home.

Which of the following creates an easement in gross?

A) Current owner
B) Former owner
C) Sheriff
D) Utility company

28

The **right of survivorship** is a feature on some types of joint ownership of property, most notably joint tenancy and tenancy in common. When jointly owned property includes a right of survivorship, the surviving owner automatically absorbs a dying owner's share of the property.

Which of the following does right of survivorship apply?

A) Life tenants
B) Joint Tenants
C) Holdover tenants
D) Tenants in common

29

Property tax is an assessed real estate tax which is usually based on the value of the property owned and is often evaluated by local or municipal governments.

Which of the following conditions deduct real estate taxes from an owner's income?

A) The property is income producing.
B) The property is in a drug-free school zone.
C) The property is in a drug-free school zone.
D) All of the above

CONTINUE ▶

30

Market value should exchange on the date of valuation between a willing buyer and a willing seller in an arms-length transaction after proper marketing wherein the parties had each acted knowledgeably, prudently.

Which of the following percentages of market value must be insured for replacement cost to be in effect?

A) 80%

B) 75%

C) 25%

D) 20%

31

An **equalization factor** is used as a multiplier to assess the value of a property to arrive at a value for the property that is in line with statewide tax assessments.

When is an equalization factor needed?

A) Where senior citizens are deserving of a lower tax rate.

B) One major company contributes most of the community's tax revenue.

C) Multiple communities contribute to a regional high school.

D) Commercial and residential properties need to be taxed at different tax rates.

32

The **Fair Housing Act** bans the refusal to rent or sell a dwelling to any person because of race, color, religion, sex, familial status, or national origin.

Which of the following does the Federal Fair Housing Act of 1968 apply?

A) Only those states that do not have state fair housing laws

B) Only people in the 15 southeastern states of the United States

C) Landlords and homeowners only

D) None of the above

33

A **Multiple Listing Service** (MLS) is a type of service used by a group of real estate brokers. They band together to create an MLS that allows each of them to see one another's listings of properties for sale.

Which of the following should a licensee immediately call upon obtaining a written offer on a MLS property?

A) MLS

B) The listing broker

C) The property owner

D) None of the above

34

Building Permit authorizes a government or other regulatory body before the construction of a new or existing building can legally occur.

Which of the following is the purpose of a building permit?

A) Ensure the community develops following the master plan.
B) Ensure sanitary conditions for septic systems are met.
C) Ensure building facades are culturally correct.
D) None of the above

35

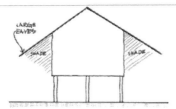

Which of the following describe the eaves of a structure in the portions of the roof?

A) Come together at the peak.
B) Allow the attic spaces to breathe.
C) Overhang the sides
D) None of the above

36

Property valuation refers to the process of developing an opinion of value for real property.

Which of the following is TRUE regarding the effects of income and expenses on property valuation?

A) Capital expenses have no effect on property value.
B) Higher profit means higher property value.
C) Lower profit means higher property value.
D) Profit has no relation to property value.

37

Housing discrimination is when an individual or a family is treated unequally when trying to buy, rent, lease, sell or finance a home based on specific characteristics, such as race, class, sex, religion, national origin, and familial status.

If there is an incident of discrimination, which of the following does the complainant need only to prove?

A) The act caused a loss.
B) The act was one act in a pattern of discrimination.
C) The act was intentional.
D) Discrimination occurred

38

Two sisters are siblings and own property as joint tenants. One of the sisters decides to sell her share to a third person for a reduced amount.

Which of the following is the correct way to address the third person upon closing?

A) Joint tenant with the sibling
B) Tenant in common with the sibling
C) Tenant by the entirety with the sibling
D) Tenant at will with the sibling

39

The **payoff statement** reflects the remaining loan balance and the number of payments and the rate of interest. It also states the amount of interest that will be rebated due to prepayment by the borrower.

Which of the following refers to paying off a loan by making installment payments?

A) Amortization
B) Habendum
C) Satisfaction
D) Usury

40

A house flipper renovates a kitchen in a city which adopts the ICC model codes.

Which of the following building codes is the flipper most concerned about for his kitchen renovation?

A) International Building Code
B) International Existing Building Code
C) International Residential Code
D) None of the answers are correct.

41

Asbestos contains any of several minerals which readily separate into long flexible fibers, that cause asbestosis and have been implicated as causes of certain cancers, and that have been used especially formerly as fireproof insulating materials.

Which of the following should only remove asbestos?

A) Licensed and bonded cleaning business
B) Licensed asbestos removal companies
C) The homeowner acting alone
D) General Contractor

42

Radon is known as a naturally occurring radioactive gas which comes from the radioactive decay of uranium. It is usually found in igneous rock and soil, but in some cases, well water may also be a source of radon.

Which of the following is true for radon gas?

A) Colorless

B) Harmful

C) Odorless

D) All of the above

43

Tax assessment determines the value, and sometimes, the use of a property to calculate a property tax.

Which of the following is the first step in contesting a property's tax assessment?

A) Meeting with the mayor

B) Meeting with the building inspector

C) Meeting with the tax assessor

D) Meeting with the tax collector

44

Which of the following is true of a Real Estate Investment Trust?

A) Each investor owns a specific property in the trust.

B) REIT's can only be sold when a property is sold.

C) The trust can only have one type of underlying investment.

D) Shareholders receive profits from rent or mortgage payments.

45

Which of the following increase in a long-term capital gain tax rate will result if a taxpayer has a marginal rate of 28%?

A) 5%

B) 10%

C) 15%

D) 20%

46

Which of the following describes recapture of depreciation?

A) The federal government forcing elderly property owners into the street

B) The state government seizing property from an unpopular person

C) The federal government recovering sheltered taxes after the sale of an investment property

D) A municipality fining property owners for unsatisfactory property maintenance

47

Which of the following should an appraiser not consider in performing an area-regional and neighborhood analysis of residential property?

A) Whether the area has a high level of conformity

B) Whether the property is located in a desirable school district

C) Whether the local economy has a variety of employment opportunities

D) Whether the area has a high ratio of real estate agents to mortgage brokers

48

Good Faith Estimate refers to an estimate of fees that is due at closing for a mortgage loan which must be provided by a lender to a borrower.

Which of the following is the number of business days which a loan applicant must receive a good faith estimate?

A) Three

B) Seven

C) Ten

D) Thirty

SECTION 1

#	Answer	Topic	Subtopic	#	Answer	Topic	Subtopic	#	Answer	Topic	Subtopic	#	Answer	Topic	Subtopic
1	D	TD	SD5	13	A	TC	SC3	25	B	TB	SB5	37	D	TB	SB2
2	B	TB	SB6	14	B	TC	SC3	26	D	TD	SD2	38	A	TB	SB4
3	A	TC	SC2	15	D	TC	SC1	27	D	TA	SA7	39	A	TA	SA7
4	C	TD	SD5	16	A	TA	SA7	28	B	TA	SA2	40	B	TB	SB3
5	A	TC	SC2	17	C	TC	SC1	29	D	TC	SC1	41	B	TD	SD1
6	B	TD	SD5	18	C	TB	SB3	30	A	TC	SC2	42	D	TD	SD1
7	D	TA	SA2	19	B	TD	SD7	31	C	TC	SC3	43	C	TB	SB6
8	D	TA	SA1	20	D	TB	SB4	32	D	TB	SB2	44	D	TD	SD4
9	D	TA	SA4	21	C	TA	SA7	33	C	TB	SB5	45	C	TC	SC1
10	D	TD	SD5	22	B	TD	SD4	34	A	TB	SB6	46	C	TC	SC1
11	B	TA	SA2	23	B	TA	SA1	35	C	TD	SD1	47	C	TA	SA7
12	C	TB	SB4	24	C	TC	SC3	36	B	TA	SA3	48	A	TD	SD2

Topics & Subtopics

Code	Description	Code	Description
SA1	Commercial Investment	SC2	Property Insurance
SA2	Estates & Interests	SC3	Taxes Assessment
SA3	Income Approach to Real Estate Valuation	SD1	Construction & Environmental Issues
SA4	Mortgage Brokerage	SD2	Deeds & Title Closing Costs
SA7	Real Estate Market	SD4	Real Estate Investment & Analysis
SB2	Human Rights & Fair Housing	SD5	The contract of sales and leases
SB3	Land Use & Regulations	SD7	Forms of Property Ownership
SB4	Law of Agency	TA	Economics
SB5	License Law	TB	Rules & Regulations
SB6	Municipal Agencies	TC	Taxes & Insurance
SC1	Income Tax Issues	TD	Transactions & Processes

TEST DIRECTION

DIRECTIONS

Read the questions carefully and then choose the ONE best answer to each question.

Be sure to allocate your time carefully so you are able to complete the entire test within the testing session. You may go back and review your answers at any time.

You may use any available space in your test booklet for scratch work.

Questions in this booklet are not actual test questions but they are the samples for commonly asked questions.

This test aims to cover all topics which may appear on the actual test. However some topics may not be covered.

Studying this booklet will be preparing you for the actual test. It will not guarantee improving your test score but it will help you pass your exam on the first attempt.

Some useful tips for answering multiple choice questions;

- Start with the questions that you can easily answer.

- Underline the keywords in the question.

- Be sure to read all the choices given.

- Watch for keywords such as NOT, always, only, all, never, completely.

- Do not forget to answer every question.

1

A landlord places a term in a lease prohibiting pets on the premises.

Which of the following types of property is illustrated?

A) Control
B) Possession
C) Title
D) Transfer

2

Which of the following refers to a tenant who defaults on a lease but remains in the premises?

A) Codicil
B) Ingrate
C) Tenant at sufferance
D) Tenant by the entirety

3

A **sales agent** sells or distributes products in a given territory but who is self-employed, takes title to the goods, and does not act as agent for a principal.

Which of the following may compensate a sales agent?

A) Customer
B) Own broker
C) Sales agent
D) Seller

4

Which of the following describes the practice of a broker depositing trust funds into the firm's operating account?

A) Commingling
B) Diversion
C) Misappropriating
D) Mingling

5

Who restricts a mortgage that requires a borrower to maintain his property in a certain way?

A) Borrower
B) Court
C) Lender
D) The government

6

Which of the following expenses should an investment property seller be able to give accurate figures?

A) Property taxes
B) Finance costs
C) Insurance
D) All of these answers are correct.

7

Which of the following can be the best source to determine the legally recognizable location and boundaries of a parcel of real estate?

A) City map

B) GIS mapping site on the Internet

C) Legal description in a deed

D) Post office

8

Which of the following binds in an option to renew?

A) Landlord

B) Tenant

C) Both A & B

D) Neither A or B

9

Tacking refers to a legal concept arising under a common law relating to competing priorities between two or more security interests arising over the same asset.

Which of the following define the process of tacking?

A) Adding successive time periods for owners and former owners to acquire an easement

B) Establishing a lien on a property through a court action

C) Filing a lis pendens with the county clerk

D) None of the above

10

Which of the following expenses are not included in calculating net operating income of a rental property?

A) Utility Fees

B) Property taxes

C) Mortgage interest

D) Insurance

11

A **circuit breaker** automatically interrupts the flow of electric current when the current goes beyond a preset limit.

Which of the following is the use of a circuit breaker?

A) Distribute electricity throughout a structure.
B) Muffle the braying of visiting in-laws.
C) Remove moisture from wiring around bathroom areas.
D) Prevent water from leaking into an attic from the chimney opening.

12

Which of the following does security deposit the seller has on hand for a tenant appear on the closing statement?

A) Debit to the seller
B) Credit to the seller
C) Neither A or B
D) Both A & B

13

Which of the following refers to the only use of lead plumbing pipes?

A) Conduits for electrical lines
B) Hot water tanks
C) Incoming water lines
D) None of the above

14

Mutual assent refers to an agreement between two parties to form a contract. It is mutual assent signifies that the parties agree to the terms they are setting, as long as the requirements are in place.

Which of the following refers to mutual assent?

A) Counteroffer
B) Fiduciary offer
C) Lawful objective
D) Meeting of the minds

15

Which of the following choices can be represented by an agent in a single agency?

A) Buyer
B) Seller
C) Both A and B
D) Neither A or B

16

Deed restrictions refer to private agreements restricting the use of the real estate and are listed in the deed. The seller may add a restriction to the title of the property.

Which of the following makes the deed restriction invalid when its right has been restricted?

A) Install a swimming pool
B) Raise horses
C) Grow crops
D) Sell the property

17

Which of the following refers to a rule or regulation passed by a local government, such as a city?

A) Code
B) Law
C) Ordinance
D) Statute

18

Which of the following does a loan originator use to determine the estimated value of a property based on an analytical comparison of similar property sales?

A) An appraisal
B) An area survey
C) A market survey
D) A cost-benefit analysis

19

The **Civil Rights Act of 1866** explains citizenship and affirms that the law equally protects all citizens.

Which of the following refers to the basis for the Civil Rights Act of 1866 that prohibits discrimination without exception?

A) National Origin
B) Race
C) Religion
D) All of the above

CONTINUE ▶

20

An **operating expense** refers to the ongoing cost for running a business, system or product.

Which of the following expenses are not included in calculating net operating expenses?

A) Property Taxes
B) Property Insurance
C) Utility Charges
D) Mortgage Interest

21

Which of the following choices is included in the fiduciary duties of a Real Estate Agent?

A) Accounting
B) Confidentiality
C) All of the above
D) None of the above

22

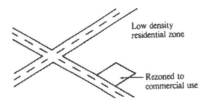

Which of the following best refers to spot zoning?

A) Illegal
B) Used primarily to bring new businesses to an area
C) Used to bring property values in line with neighboring parcels of property
D) A use for land that is totally in harmony with the surrounding neighborhoods

23

Which of the following refers to the combining of two or more parcels of land into one tract that has higher total value than the sum of individual plots?

A) Affirmative easement
B) Plottage
C) Plot planting
D) Undue influence

24

The **HUD-1 Settlement Statement** was to itemize fees and services charged to the borrower by the broker or lender to apply for a loan for purchasing or refinancing real estate. HUD refers to the Department of Housing and Urban Development.

How long must the parties to a real estate closing be given on reviewing the HUD statement?

A) 3 hours
B) 12 hours
C) 24 hours
D) Three days

25

Which of the following scenario will exclude a commission payment in an exclusive right to sell agreement?

A) The property is not sold
B) The property is sold by the seller
C) The property is sold by a cooperating broker
D) The property is sold by an uncooperative broker

26

A 5-acre parcel of land was sold for $14,750,000. Which of the following was the price per square foot (ft2)?

A) $17.70
B) $67.70
C) $338.60
D) $677.70

27

The **income approach** refers to a real estate appraisal method allowing to estimate the value of a property by taking the net operating income of the rent collected and dividing it by the capitalization rate.

Which of the following kinds of buyer does the income approach to property valuation is useful?

A) First-time homebuyer
B) Flipper
C) Rental real estate investor
D) Retirees

Which of the following conditions should only exist for a broker/sales-person to assist a homeowner in renting the upstairs unit of a two-family home to a person of Polish origin?

A) The broker receives the commission from the tenant.

B) An upstairs unit is a legal unit.

C) The upstairs unit has a separate entrance.

D) None of the above

Which of the following refers to the act of giving the property to a municipal government for public use?

A) Regurgitation

B) Dedication

C) Gestation

D) Grantation

A **rate of return** refers to the loss or gain on an investment over a specified period in the percentage of the investment's cost.

Which of the following is the rate of return of a building earning $180,000 annually that had a purchase price of $1,750,000?

A) 12.4%

B) 124%

C) 15%

D) 10.3%

A **single-detached dwelling** is a free-standing residential building. Sometimes referred to as a single family home as opposed to a multi-family residential dwelling.

Which of the following is the most common appraisal approach used in appraising single-family housing?

A) Sales comparison approach

B) Rental approach

C) Income approach

D) Cost approach

32

Encroachment is where a property owner violates the property rights of his neighbor such as building something on the neighbor's land or allowing something to hang over onto the neighbor's property.

Which of the following could be the least advisable path to take with regards to encroachment on your property?

A) Do nothing.

B) Sue for trespass.

C) Give an easement for encroachment.

D) Sell the property where the encroachment sits to the owner of the encroachment.

33

Capital expense refers to the money a company spends to buy, maintain, or improve its fixed assets, such as buildings, vehicles, equipment, or land.

Which of the following describes an example of a capital expense that should be considered in property valuation?

A) Fixed rate mortgage payment

B) Property taxes

C) Roof replacement allowance

D) Vacancy

34

Your neighbor has started to raise pigs in his suburban yard which in turn, stinking up your yard. There are no restrictive covenants or equitable servitudes that apply.

Which of the following is your best way to make the neighbor stop if he won't do so voluntarily utilizing a private method?

A) File a private nuisance lawsuit.

B) Obtain an easement.

C) Have the city condemn the property.

D) There's no private solution available.

35

Which of the following is the annual taxes on a property with an assessed value of $750,000 and a tax rate of $2.20 per thousand dollars of assessed value?

A) $1050

B) $1,650

C) $16500

D) $10500

36

Which of the following is the gross income multiplier of a house that rents for $1,200 each month and would sell for $150,000?

A) 120

B) 125

C) 130

D) 300

37

The **Condominium Act** states that the unit owners association and its board must comply with the act and with the condominium's bylaws, rules, and regulations.

Which of the following is/are the by-laws of a condominium development?

A) Regulations by which the Association manages the development

B) Only a formality to get municipal approvals for the development

C) Not given to purchasers until binding contracts are signed

D) None of the above

38

A home with a market value of $3,100,000 is insured for 75% of its market value.

If the cost of insurance is $2.03 per $1,000 of insured value, which of the following is the monthly cost of insurance for this home?

A) $389.80

B) $393.30

C) $524.40

D) $4,719.80

39

A **covenant**, in real property law, is used for conditions tied to the use of land.

Which of the following enforce a covenant in a deed?

A) Court order

B) Habendum clause

C) Local police

D) The condo association

40

Which of the following refers to the organization that develops a set of international building code standards adopted by many states and local governments in the United States?

A) The IMF
B) The World Bank
C) The ICC
D) The UN

41

Multifamily residential refers to multiple separate housing units for residential inhabitants contained in one building or several buildings within one complex.

Which of the following appraisal approaches would appraise multifamily apartment building?

A) Income approach
B) Market data
C) Cost
D) All of the above

42

A **certificate of occupancy** refers to a document issued by a local government agency to certify a building's compliance with applicable building codes and other laws and indicating it to be in a condition suitable for occupancy.

Which of the following conditions will issue a Certificate of Occupancy?

A) When the tax assessor determines the value of the home improvement
B) When a construction job passes the final inspection of the building inspector
C) Only after approved plans are submitted
D) When a home improvement application is submitted to the building inspector

43

The **mortgage's principal and interest payment** is the main component of a monthly mortgage payment. The principal is the amount borrowed and had to be paid back, and interest is what the lender charges for lending money.

Which of the following does mortgage interest and principal payments constitute?

A) Cash flow
B) Debt service
C) Vacancy factor
D) Variable expenses

CONTINUE ▶

44

Economic obsolescence refers to a form of depreciation due to unfavorable external conditions to the property such as the local economy, encroachment of objectionable enterprises, and other factors.

Which of the following describes an example of economic obsolescence?

A) An outmoded air conditioning system

B) A junkyard down the block

C) A dilapidated roof

D) None of the above

45

A **Planning and Zoning Commission** refers to locally elected or appointed government board charged with recommending to the local town or city council the boundaries of the various original zoning district and appropriate regulations to be enforced.

To dispute a decision of the planning board, which of the following should a citizen go?

A) Architectural review board

B) Building inspector

C) Ombudsman

D) Zoning board of appeals

46

PITI refers to a mortgage payment which is the sum of monthly principal, interest, taxes, and insurance.

Which of the following maximum monthly PITI payments would qualify a borrower having a weekly income of $2,150 under the 28% housing ratio guideline?

A) $2,312.19

B) $2,408.00

C) $2,512.35

D) $2,608.67

47

A property initially purchased for $1,000,000 increased in value by 7% per year for three years.

Which of the following was the value of the property after the third year?

A) $1,225,043

B) $1,210,000

C) $1,200,000

D) $1,230,000

An investor requires a 15.5% rate of return. A listed property priced at $1,550,000 has a monthly income of $74,560 and monthly expenses of $54,980.

Does the property meet the investor's requirement? What should the offering price be to meet the demand?

A) Yes. $1,478,765.30
B) No. $1,478,765.30
C) No. $1,515,870.90
D) No. $1,483,671.15

SECTION 2

#	Answer	Topic	Subtopic	#	Answer	Topic	Subtopic	#	Answer	Topic	Subtopic	#	Answer	Topic	Subtopic
1	A	TD	SD7	13	D	TD	SD1	25	A	TB	SB4	37	A	TB	SB1
2	C	TD	SD5	14	D	TD	SD5	26	B	TA	SA6	38	B	TA	SA6
3	B	TA	SA7	15	B	TB	SB4	27	C	TA	SA3	39	A	TB	SB3
4	A	TB	SB5	16	D	TA	SA1	28	D	TB	SB2	40	C	TB	SB3
5	C	TB	SB3	17	C	TB	SB3	29	B	TD	SD2	41	A	TD	SD6
6	A	TD	SD4	18	A	TD	SD4	30	D	TA	SA1	42	B	TB	SB6
7	C	TA	SA7	19	B	TB	SB2	31	A	TA	SA3	43	B	TA	SA5
8	A	TD	SD5	20	D	TD	SD4	32	A	TD	SD7	44	B	TD	SD3
9	A	TA	SA2	21	D	TB	SB5	33	C	TA	SA3	45	D	TB	SB6
10	C	TD	SD6	22	C	TB	SB3	34	A	TB	SB3	46	D	TA	SA5
11	A	TD	SD1	23	B	TD	SD4	35	B	TD	SD6	47	A	TA	SA1
12	A	TD	SD2	24	C	TD	SD5	36	B	TA	SA3	48	C	TA	SA5

Topics & Subtopics

Code	Description	Code	Description
SA1	Commercial Investment	SB6	Municipal Agencies
SA2	Estates & Interests	SD1	Construction & Environmental Issues
SA3	Income Approach to Real Estate Valuation	SD2	Deeds & Title Closing Costs
SA5	Real Estate Finance	SD3	Property Management
SA6	Real Estate Math	SD4	Real Estate Investment & Analysis
SA7	Real Estate Market	SD5	The contract of sales and leases
SB1	Condominiums & Suites	SD6	Valuation
SB2	Human Rights & Fair Housing	SD7	Forms of Property Ownership
SB3	Land Use & Regulations	TA	Economics
SB4	Law of Agency	TB	Rules & Regulations
SB5	License Law	TD	Transactions & Processes

CONTINUE ▶

TEST DIRECTION

Read the questions carefully and then choose the ONE best answer to each question.

Be sure to allocate your time carefully so you are able to complete the entire test within the testing session. You may go back and review your answers at any time.

You may use any available space in your test booklet for scratch work.

Questions in this booklet are not actual test questions but they are the samples for commonly asked questions.

This test aims to cover all topics which may appear on the actual test. However some topics may not be covered.

Studying this booklet will be preparing you for the actual test. It will not guarantee improving your test score but it will help you pass your exam on the first attempt.

Some useful tips for answering multiple choice questions;

- Start with the questions that you can easily answer.

- Underline the keywords in the question.

- Be sure to read all the choices given.

- Watch for keywords such as NOT, always, only, all, never, completely.

- Do not forget to answer every question.

1

Which of the following should be the form of an expressed agreement?

A) Oral
B) In writing
C) Binding on both parties
D) All of the above

2

A **printed circuit board** (PCB) is to support and connect electronic parts using conductive pads, tracks and other properties etched from copper sheets laminated onto a non-conductive substrate.

Which of the following do PCBs usually found?

A) Aerosol cans
B) Heating Units
C) Cooling Systems
D) Electrical equipment

3

A **commercial lease** is for tenants using the property for commercial purposes such as business versus residential use.

At the end of a commercial lease, which of the following does the trade fixtures belong?

A) Tenant
B) Landlord
C) Agent
D) None of the above

4

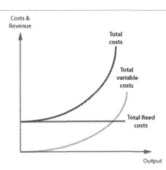

Variable cost refers to an expense that varies with production output. Variable costs are those costs that vary depending on volume; they rise as production increases and fall as production decreases. Variable costs differ from fixed costs.

Which of the following is most likely be a variable expense?

A) Taxes
B) Heating fuel
C) None of the above
D) None of the above

5

Which of the following is the type of document that is issued when an improvement has been made to a property and the building inspector has passed it?

A) Deed

B) Tax assessment

C) Building permit

D) Certificate of Occupancy

6

An **assessed value** refers to the value assigned to a property to measure applicable taxes.

Which of the following determines the assessed value of a property?

A) Tax Assessor

B) Tax Collector

C) Planning board

D) Municipal council

7

Which of the following can describe a non-conforming use?

A) It is illegal

B) It must be removed or closed if it changes owners

C) It was in existence prior to zoning laws being created

D) None of the above

8

Condemnation suit is a judicial proceeding to take property by eminent domain for public use upon the payment of just compensation for such taking.

Which of the following is the condition when a condemnation suit is filed against a property owner?

A) Escheat

B) Downzoning

C) Eminent Domain

D) Use variance

9

Deed refers to a legal document which is an official record and proof of ownership of property.

Which of the following is needed for a deed to be valid?

A) Be in triplicate

B) Be signed by the grantor

C) Be signed by the grantee

D) All of the above

10

Security means any written, electronic or oral agreement that is secured by any lien or charge upon the capital, assets, profits, property or credit of any person or any public or governmental body, subdivision, or agency.

Which of the following refers to security in a real state?

A) An apartment building owned in a partnership

B) Real estate investment trust shares

C) None of the above

D) All of the above

11

Which type of consideration does a lot with a fantastic view of the ocean have?

A) Economic

B) Government

C) Physical

D) Social

12

Which of the following organizations establishes a National Register of Historic Places?

A) CERCLA

B) NEPA

C) National Registry Act of 1968

D) None of the answers are correct.

13

Which of the following is the term appropriate in the situation where an agent is following the lawful instructions of a client?

A) Care

B) Loyalty

C) Obedience

D) Accounting

14

Mary has the right to use a path which crosses her neighbor's property to reach a public street.

Which of the following is the best description of her property right?

A) Adverse possession

B) Control

C) Easement

D) Possession

15

Which of the following refers to the document that creates a relationship between a property owner and a broker?

A) New York State Property Manager License

B) Management agreement

C) Operating statement

D) Rent roll

16

An **open market** is an unrestricted market with free access by and competition of buyers and sellers.

Which of the following refers to the most probable price a property would be sold for an open market?

A) Appraised value

B) Cost

C) Market Value

D) Seller's value

17

A **minor** under the law refers to a person under a certain age that is usually the age of majority which is the shift from childhood to adulthood. Generally, the age of majority is 18 but also depends upon jurisdiction and application.

Which of the following is a contract entered into by a minor?

A) Voidable

B) Void

C) Valid

D) Exculpatory

18

Which of the following do state laws allow a landlord to refuse to rent?

A) Rock musician

B) People with dogs

C) Someone on welfare

D) All of the above

19

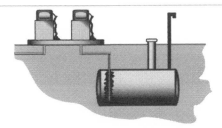

Which of the following describes the primary risk to the environment from underground storage tanks?

A) Ruptured tanks leaking toxic materials

B) Wildlife drinking from the open ends

C) The emission of fumes into the air from faulty vents

D) None of the above

20

Which of the following definitions can market value best define in a property?

A) Most probable selling price

B) Most recent selling price

C) Listing price

D) Appraised value for property tax purposes

21

Which of the following is issued by a local government indicating that a building is fit for human occupation?

A) Building code

B) Occupancy permit

C) Title

D) Warranty of habitability

22

A property with dimensions of 125 x 200 sold for $1,750,000.

Which of the following was the price of the property per front foot?

A) $70.00
B) $1,400.00
C) $8,750.00
D) $14,000.00

23

When Bernard bought his property, he had a 20% down payment and secured a 30-year loan at 7% interest.

If his first month's interest was $2240.00, how much did he pay for the property?

A) $260,000
B) $290,000
C) $410,000
D) $480,000

24

Mila is looking to buy a property which costs $115,000 and can rent for $750 per month. She has done some research and has determined the net operating expenses to be $5,000 per year. Her desired cap rate is 7%.

Which of the following is the appraisal value of this property rounded to the nearest dollar using the income capitalization approach?

A) $34,000
B) $57,143
C) $83,333
D) $106,950

25

Conservative investing refers to an investing strategy seeking to preserve an investment portfolio's value by investing in lower risk securities.

Which of the following should an investor consider to conserve capital?

A) Regional shopping malls
B) Industrial parks
C) Highly leveraged properties
D) Fee simple purchases

26

Which of the following persons is required in state real property laws to have a real estate license?

A) Auctioneer
B) Executor
C) Practicing Attorney
D) None of the above

27

Which of the following is the definition of adverse possession?

A) Giving up property voluntarily to the government
B) A legal proceeding to divide property owned by two or more people
C) The sudden loss of land by an act of nature like a landslide
D) When someone uses your property for a period of time, and you lose the property or have your rights to the property restricted

28

Which of the following refers to a public restriction on how a person can use his/her land situated in a particular area of town?

A) Easement
B) Profit a pendre
C) Restrictive covenant
D) Zoning ordinance

29

Interested house buyer can often approach a lender, and the lender can provide assurances they would be able to get a loan up to a certain amount.

Which of the following is involved in a pre-approval letter?

A) An application that is made under oath
B) An underwriter's affidavit
C) Bonding of the borrowers
D) Verification of employment and credit history

CONTINUE ▶

30

A parcel of property having an area of 2,356,000 square feet has a width of 3100 feet.

How deep is the property?

A) 760 Feet

B) 890 Feet

C) 2350 Feet

D) 3100 Feet

31

Ana's house is the eldest home in her neighborhood. However, her property has been valued higher than she expected.

Which of the following principles of valuation is likely at play?

A) Principle of progression

B) Principle of contribution

C) Principle of regression

D) Principle of highest and best use

32

A **transfer tax** refers to a tax on the passing of property title to another person.

Which of the following do transfer taxes are usually the closing cost?

A) Closing Attorney

B) Lender

C) Seller

D) Buyer

33

Zeus imparts a part of his real property to Chris so long as the property is for residential purposes; if it ceases to be used for residential purposes, Brent will receive the property in fee simple.

What type of future interest does Brent have?

A) A contingent remainder

B) A vested remainder

C) A reversion

D) An executory interest

34

A **mortgage broker** works with a borrower and a lender to qualify the borrower for a mortgage.

Which of the following may compensate mortgage broker?

A) The lender

B) The borrower

C) Neither A or B

D) Both A and B

35

A lot that measures 840' x 670' sold for $2,532,600. Which of the following was the cost per square foot?

A) $4.50

B) $4.25

C) $2.75

D) $2.50

CONTINUE ▶

36

Earnest money refers to a deposit made to a seller showing the buyer's good faith in a transaction.

Which of the following does an earnest money deposit appear on a closing statement?

A) Debit to seller

B) Debit to buyer

C) Credit to seller

D) Credit to buyer

37

An investment property's monthly net income is $16,540, and its monthly operating expenses are $9,230.

If the investor paid $750,500 for the property, which of the following is the investor's rate of return?

A) 1.2%

B) 8.7%

C) 11.7%

D) 13.9%

38

Kristine has offered to purchase Clyde's house which has pending results of a property inspection. The report indicates that the roof needs to be repaired. Kristine asks Clyde to fix the roof.

Which of the following is NOT a viable option for Clyde?

A) Offer a lower purchase price.

B) Refuse to make the repairs.

C) Refuse and keep the earnest money.

D) Repair the roof.

39

Torrens title is a type of land registration which a register of land holdings maintained by the state guarantees an indefeasible title to those included in the register.

Which of the following investigates the title to a parcel of property seeking to be registered in a state that uses the Torrens Title System?

A) A judge

B) A retained attorney

C) The Examiner of Title

D) The Registrar of Title

CONTINUE ▶

40

Which of the following may compensate a residential apartment building manager?

A) Kickbacks from maintenance service companies

B) Key money

C) Percentage of collected rents

D) Rebates from fuel oil suppliers

41

Which of the following is the process undertaken under the National Historic Preservation Act concerning the assessment of a proposed project involving a property listed on the National Register of Historic Places?

A) EAS

B) EIS

C) Section 106 review

D) None of the answers are correct.

42

In the United States, a **historic district** is a group of buildings, properties, or sites that have been designated by one of several entities on different levels as historically or architecturally significant.

Which of the following historic areas usually need permission to alter?

A) Dining areas

B) Plumbing fixtures

C) Interior of a building

D) The exterior of a building

43

Collateral is a property or asset that a borrower offers as a way for a lender to secure the loan.

Which of the following collaterals is needed for a co-op purchaser to purchase a loan?

A) Co-op building stock

B) Bond

C) Property deed

D) Title policy

44

National Environmental Policy Act (NEPA) is an environmental law imposed in the United States to promote the enhancement of the environment and established the President's Council on Environmental Quality (CEQ).

Which of the following refers to a report issued under NEPA on a proposed project?

A) EIS

B) Environmental Assessment Statement

C) Section 106 report

D) None of the answers are correct.

45

Which of the following will happen to an apartment under a lease that becomes unusable due to smoke from a fire in an adjacent unit?

A) The landlord's responsibility to immediately terminate the lease

B) The requirement of the tenant to remain in the apartment until it is condemned

C) Termed an actual eviction

D) Termed a constructive eviction

46

Police power refers to the ability of the states to regulate behavior and enforce order within their territory for the betterment of the health, safety, morals, and general welfare of their inhabitants.

Which one of the following is not a land use regulation enacted according to the police power?

A) Zoning ordinances

B) Historic districts

C) Building codes

D) None of the answers are correct.

47

A **mortgage broker** acts as a person in between a client and a bank to review the client's financial ability to pay off a potential mortgage and decide if they are financially established enough for the bank to back their real estate purchase.

Which of the following does mortgage broker mostly involve?

A) Originating loan applications

B) Providing the mortgage loan funds

C) Property value determination

D) All of the above

A salesperson sold a property listed for $2,999,000 for $2,830,000. The selling broker's commission was 40% of the 6% commission paid by the owner, and the salesperson received 45% of the selling broker's split of the commission.

After buying a brass doorknocker for the new homeowners valued at $190.50, how much money will the agent take home?

A) $3,560.90

B) 3,219.40

C) $3,056.40

D) $3,036.90

SECTION 3

#	Answer	Topic	Subtopic	#	Answer	Topic	Subtopic	#	Answer	Topic	Subtopic	#	Answer	Topic	Subtopic
1	D	TB	SB4	13	C	TB	SB4	25	B	TA	SA1	37	C	TA	SA3
2	D	TD	SD1	14	C	TD	SD7	26	A	TB	SB5	38	C	TA	SA7
3	A	TD	SD5	15	B	TD	SD3	27	D	TB	SB6	39	C	TD	SD7
4	B	TD	SD3	16	C	TD	SD3	28	D	TA	SA7	40	C	TD	SD3
5	B	TB	SB3	17	A	TD	SD5	29	D	TA	SA6	41	C	TB	SB3
6	A	TB	SB3	18	D	TB	SB2	30	A	TA	SA6	42	D	TB	SB6
7	C	TB	SB3	19	A	TD	SD1	31	A	TA	SA7	43	A	TB	SB1
8	C	TB	SB3	20	A	TA	SA7	32	C	TD	SD2	44	A	TB	SB3
9	B	TD	SD2	21	B	TB	SB3	33	B	TD	SD7	45	D	TD	SD5
10	B	TD	SD4	22	D	TA	SA1	34	D	TA	SA4	46	D	TB	SB3
11	C	TA	SA1	23	D	TA	SA4	35	A	TA	SA2	47	A	TA	SA5
12	D	TB	SB3	24	B	TA	SA3	36	D	TD	SD2	48	D	TA	SA6

Topics & Subtopics

Code	Description	Code	Description
SA1	Commercial Investment	SB5	License Law
SA2	Estates & Interests	SB6	Municipal Agencies
SA3	Income Approach to Real Estate Valuation	SD1	Construction & Environmental Issues
SA4	Mortgage Brokerage	SD2	Deeds & Title Closing Costs
SA5	Real Estate Finance	SD3	Property Management
SA6	Real Estate Math	SD4	Real Estate Investment & Analysis
SA7	Real Estate Market	SD5	The contract of sales and leases
SB1	Condominiums & Suites	SD7	Forms of Property Ownership
SB2	Human Rights & Fair Housing	TA	Economics
SB3	Land Use & Regulations	TB	Rules & Regulations
SB4	Law of Agency	TD	Transactions & Processes

CONTINUE ▶

TEST DIRECTION

Read the questions carefully and then choose the ONE best answer to each question.

Be sure to allocate your time carefully so you are able to complete the entire test within the testing session. You may go back and review your answers at any time.

You may use any available space in your test booklet for scratch work.

Questions in this booklet are not actual test questions but they are the samples for commonly asked questions.

This test aims to cover all topics which may appear on the actual test. However some topics may not be covered.

Studying this booklet will be preparing you for the actual test. It will not guarantee improving your test score but it will help you pass your exam on the first attempt.

Some useful tips for answering multiple choice questions;

- Start with the questions that you can easily answer.

- Underline the keywords in the question.

- Be sure to read all the choices given.

- Watch for keywords such as NOT, always, only, all, never, completely.

- Do not forget to answer every question.

CONTINUE ▶

1

Which of the following describes the part of a lease that states the intention of the lessor and the lessee?

A) Habitability clause
B) Demising clause
C) Usage clause
D) Santa clause

2

An **elected official** refers to a person who is an official by an election. Which of the following are not elected?

A) City Council members
B) Board of Trustee members
C) Planning Board members
D) Town Council members

3

Which of the following state laws protect investors from a lack of vetted information?

A) Blank Slate Laws
B) Blue Sky Laws
C) The Securities Act of 1933
D) None of these answers are correct.

4

Which of the following is the massive wooden members that sit atop the foundation wall and upon which the frame is placed?

A) Girders
B) Joists
C) Bridging
D) Sills

5

A **feasibility study** refers to an analysis of the success of a project's completion, accounting for factors like economic, technological, legal and scheduling. Project managers use feasibility studies to study the positive and negative outcomes of a project before investing.

Which of the following does a feasibility study in Real Estate determine?

A) Whether undertaking the investment or not
B) The location for a successful venture
C) The value of an investment property
D) None of the above

44

CONTINUE ▶

The **assessment rate** refers to a uniform percentage and varies by tax jurisdiction, and could be any percentage below 100%. After getting the assessed value, it is multiplied by the mill levy to determine your taxes due

Which of the following is the role of municipal tax assessor?

A) Sets the tax collector's goals

B) Determines the value of properties in the community

C) Determines the tax rate property owners pay

D) Collects taxes from property owners

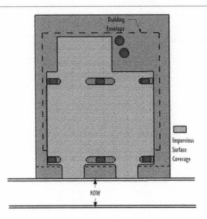

Setbacks refer to the imposed building restrictions on property owners. Local governments create setbacks through ordinances and Building Codes, usually for reasons of public policy such as safety, privacy, and environmental protection.

Which of the following refers to the setback?

A) Judgment

B) Sheathing

C) Disappointment

D) Mandated distance

8

The **binding contract** refers to an agreement in writing between two or more individuals which a court can impose penalties in the event one negates to his/her promise as outlined in the contract.

Which of the following must be given to a person before signing a binding contract to purchase a condominium?

A) Bond

B) Blank contract

C) Public Offering Statement

D) Survey

9

Which of the following is a contract that binds in only one party?

A) Binder

B) Unilateral contract

C) Bilateral contract

D) Implied contract

10

Which of the following does a purchaser need to produce at the closing?

A) One year homeowner insurance policy

B) Deed to the property

C) Tenant lease

D) Certificate of Occupancy

11

Licensee refers to a person or business that holds an approved license to conduct an activity, such as operating a business.

Which of the following can a licensee share an earned commission?

A) Seller

B) Customer

C) No one

D) Postal worker providing a lead

CONTINUE ▶

12

Lead refers to a naturally occurring element which is found in small amounts in the earth's crust.

Which of the following must the EPA booklet entitled Protect Your Family from Lead in Your Home be given?

A) Everyone
B) Brokers
C) Sellers
D) Purchasers

13

Property management refers to the control, oversight, and operation of real estate. Management describes the need to be cared for, monitored and accounted for its useful life and condition.

Which of the following documents does a real estate broker prepare to obtain a property management job?

A) Management proposal
B) Property survey and deed analysis
C) Financial statement
D) Management proposal

14

A **septic tank** is a chamber usually underground which domestic wastewater flows for basic treatment.

Which of the following agencies requires to have well and septic systems?

A) Department of Taxation
B) State Department of Environmental Conservation
C) Department of Health
D) Environmental Protection Agency

15

A **community** describes a group of people living in the same place or having a particular characteristic in common.

Which of the following should a board create to develop a community?

A) Architectural review board
B) Board of trustees
C) Building department
D) Master plan

16

Property valuation refers to the process of creating an opinion of value for real property.

Which of the following is not one of the four foundational elements of property valuation?

A) Demand
B) Supply
C) Transferability
D) All of these are elements of property valuation.

17

Which of the following correctly describes a dual agency?

A) A real estate broker operating two real estate offices
B) Illegal without knowledge and consent of both parties
C) A combination of real estate and insurance being offered at the same time
D) A method whereby two sales agents split a commission on a transaction

18

Licensee refers to a person or business that holds an approved license to conduct an activity, such as operating a business.

Which of the following must a do when a licensee is selling his or her property?

A) Opens up the fact that he or she is a licensed real estate agent to prospective buyers
B) List the property at a fair market value
C) List the property with the MLS
D) All of the above

19

Four unities are four conditions which are required for the formation of a joint tenancy.

Which of the following is the last component of the four unities completing time, title and possession?

A) Incontinence
B) Interest
C) Loyalty
D) Trust

20

Site analysis refers to a preliminary phase of architectural and urban design processes dedicated to the study of the climatic, geographical, historical, legal, and infrastructural context of a specific site.

Which of the following does not belong to the physical factors considered in performing a site analysis?

A) Encroachments

B) Shape

C) Size

D) Zoning

21

Net operating income describes a calculation used in analyzing real estate investments that generate income.

Which of the following are some sources of revenue for calculating the net operating income?

A) Parking fees

B) Rent payments

C) Vending machine profits

D) All of these are correct answers.

22

A **property inspection** is an inspection of a building by professionally trained and experienced in evaluating buildings and their components.

During a professional property inspection, which of the following is NOT inspected?

A) Foundation

B) Heating

C) Land

D) All of these are inspected.

23

Which of the following is granted by a deed wherein the property may revert to the grantor of the deed if the condition is not be met by the grantee of the deed?

A) Indefeasible fee

B) Defeasible fee

C) Fee simple

D) None of the answers are correct.

24

Which of the following refers to the right of a government to arrest and imprison any suspicious person?

A) Police Power
B) Escheat
C) Eminent Domain
D) None of the above

25

Cooperative housing is a type of home ownership in which you own a part of a corporation that owns the building.

Which of the following income is not considered on a loan application for a cooperative unit purchase?

A) Social Security
B) Gambling
C) Commissions
D) Alimony

26

'**Federal Agencies**' are special government organizations that set up for a specific purpose such as the management of resources, financial oversight of industries or national security issues.

Which of the following is the federal agency concerned with environmental matters?

A) DEC
B) EPA
C) FHA
D) SOB

27

Which of the following choices should be fulfilled for the federal government to accept a sales agent as an independent contractor?

A) The agent earns no money
B) The agent has another job
C) The agent works out of his or her own home
D) The agent is paid strictly on a commission basis

28

Which of the following follows the correct formula for rate of return?

A) (Investment Gain - Investment Cost) / Investment Cost = Rate of Return`

B) Investment Gain / Investment Cost = Rate of Return

C) (Investment Gain + Investment Cost) / Investment Cost = Rate of Return

D) (Investment Gain -Investment Cost) / Investment Gain = Rate of Return

29

A **real estate investment trust** (REIT) means that a company operates or finances income-producing real estate.

Which of the following describes the process of taxing REIT dividends?

A) REIT dividends tax at corporate income tax rates.

B) Dividends tax at capital gains rates.

C) Investors will pay taxes on dividends at the maximum federal income tax rate.

D) Investors pay taxes on dividends at their income tax rate.

30

Which of the following is the basis that a landlord may not solely refuse a tenant?

A) Prison record

B) Political affiliation

C) Children in the family

D) All of the above

31

Which of the following ownership form exists when a corporation owns real estate?

A) By the entirety

B) In trust

C) Tenants in common

D) In severalty

32

Mechanic's lien refers to a guarantee of payment to builders, contractors and construction firms that build or repair structures. Mechanic's liens also extend to suppliers of materials and subcontractors and cover building repairs as well.

Which of the following is where mechanics lien place on property?

A) Administrator

B) Former owner

C) Home improvement contractor

D) Owner

33

Tax deduction refers to a reduction of income which is taxed and commonly a result of expenses from those incurred to produce additional income.

Which of the following may homeowner take an income tax deduction?

A) Real estate taxes

B) Mortgage interest paid

C) None of the above

D) All of the above

34

When Bernard bought his property, he had a 20% down payment and secured a 30-year loan at 7% interest.

If his first month's interest was $2240.00, how much did he pay for the property?

A) $480,000

B) $410,000

C) $290,000

D) $260,000

35

Which of the following is required to qualify as a limited partnership?

A) At least one general partner and one limited partner

B) Two or more limited partners and an annual franchise fee paid to the state

C) At least two general partners and registration with the state

D) At least two general partners

36

You referred a client to a lender. In return they sent you a thank you note with a $100 gift card to a local restaurant.

Which of the following law makes this kickback illegal?

A) CRA

B) ECOA

C) RESPA

D) Regulation Z

37

David and Erika live in a state which recognizes dower and courtesy and also has enacted a statute entitling a surviving spouse an elective share of the deceased spouse's estate. Dave decides to disinherit Erika.

Which of the following is correct?

A) Erika loses her dower interest because David disinherited her.

B) Erika may elect the rightful share or claim her dower interest.

C) Erika loses her right to an elective share because she has been disinherited by will.

D) None of the answers are correct.

38

A rental property brings in $500 a month in rent and has annual net operating expenses of $2,500.

Which of the following is the net operating income of this property?

A) $2,000

B) $3,000

C) $3,500

D) None of these answers are correct.

39

A **property tax** or also called **millage rate** is a tax on the value of a property levied by the governing authority of the jurisdiction in the location of the property.

Which of the following impacts does depreciation have on real estate taxation?

A) Depreciation adds up to the basis and is only essential for taxes when the property is sold.

B) Depreciation refers to the total of all maintenance expenses associated with an aging house.

C) Depreciation lets the owner in taking a paper loss against the income of the property.

D) Depreciation lowers land value for local property taxes.

CONTINUE ▶

Which of the following refers to the general term in real estate that means a person legally owns a piece of real estate and has the right to use and enjoy it?

A) Equitable title
B) Legal title
C) Title
D) All of the answers are correct.

A **first mortgage** refers to a mortgage in a first lien position on the property that secures the mortgage. A first mortgage has priority over all other liens or claims on a property in the event of default.

Which of the following are highest priority liens?

A) Tax liens
B) Commercial liens
C) Mortgage liens
D) None of the above

A **loan** refers to borrowed money, property or other material goods in exchange for future repayment of the loan value amount along with interest.

Which of the following loans do not ensure or guarantee borrowers by the US Government?

A) Conventional loans
B) FHA loans
C) VA loans
D) None of the above

43

Zoning is a type of restriction on the way land within its jurisdiction can be used. It is through community planning and development that zoning laws help local governmental agencies preserve property values and ensure communities are functional and safe places.

Which of the following is not affected by Zoning?

A) Private property

B) The interior of a building

C) The number of parking spaces for a fast food restaurant

D) The distance a structure may be erected from a property line

44

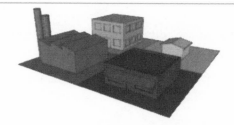

Zoning refers to the division of land in a municipality into zones in which specific land uses are permitted or prohibited.

Which of the following types of zoning would be most appropriate for a mall or a group of stores?

A) Agriculture

B) Commercial

C) Residential

D) Rural

45

A **life estate** refers to the land ownership for a person's lifetime in common and statutory law. However, in legal terms, it is an estate that will terminate at death in which a property can transfer to another person or revert to the original owner.

Which of the following can life estate get created?

A) Only a relative

B) Any person

C) Only a trustee

D) None of the above

46

Ryan presents an offer to purchase Maria's house. He includes a provision which states that he can terminate the contract if an inspection reveals that necessary repairs to the house will exceed one percent of the purchase price.

Which of the following is the best description of this clause?

A) A cost of repair clause

B) An escape clause

C) An inspection clause

D) None of the answers are correct.

47

The **income approach** refers to a real estate appraisal method that allows investors to estimate the value of a property by taking the net operating income of the rent collected and dividing it by the capitalization rate.

Which of the following is a method in the income approach to property valuation?

A) Direct capitalization

B) Discounted cash flow

C) Gross income multiplier

D) All of these are correct.

48

A **cash flow statement** refers to the financial statement showing the changes in balance sheet accounts and how income affects cash and cash equivalents, and breaks the analysis down to operating, investing and financing activities.

Which of the following is the correct formula for the total cash flow statement?

A) Rental Cash Statement + Investing Cash Statement + Financing Cash Statement

B) Operations Cash Statement + Investing Cash Statement + Financing Cash Statement

C) Operations Cash Statement + Purchase Cash Statement + Sale Cash Statement

D) Operations Cash Statement + Tax Cash Statement + Financing Cash Statement

SECTION 4

#	Answer	Topic	Subtopic	#	Answer	Topic	Subtopic	#	Answer	Topic	Subtopic	#	Answer	Topic	Subtopic
1	B	TD	SD5	13	D	TD	SD3	25	B	TB	SB1	37	B	TD	SD7
2	C	TB	SB2	14	C	TD	SD1	26	B	TD	SD1	38	C	TA	SA3
3	B	TD	SD4	15	D	TB	SB6	27	D	TB	SB4	39	C	TD	SD4
4	D	TD	SD1	16	B	TA	SA2	28	A	TD	SD4	40	C	TD	SD7
5	A	TA	SA1	17	C	TB	SB4	29	D	TD	SD4	41	A	TA	SA2
6	B	TB	SB6	18	A	TB	SB5	30	C	TB	SB2	42	A	TA	SA5
7	D	TB	SB3	19	B	TA	SA2	31	D	TA	SA1	43	A	TB	SB3
8	C	TB	SB1	20	D	TA	SA2	32	C	TA	SA2	44	B	TB	SB3
9	B	TD	SD5	21	D	TA	SA3	33	D	TA	SA5	45	B	TA	SA2
10	D	TD	SD2	22	D	TA	SA7	34	A	TA	SA2	46	A	TA	SA7
11	C	TB	SB5	23	B	TB	SB3	35	A	TD	SD4	47	D	TA	SA3
12	D	TD	SD1	24	D	TB	SB3	36	C	TB	SB5	48	B	TD	SD4

Topics & Subtopics

Code	Description	Code	Description
SA1	Commercial Investment	SB6	Municipal Agencies
SA2	Estates & Interests	SD1	Construction & Environmental Issues
SA3	Income Approach to Real Estate Valuation	SD2	Deeds & Title Closing Costs
SA5	Real Estate Finance	SD3	Property Management
SA7	Real Estate Market	SD4	Real Estate Investment & Analysis
SB1	Condominiums & Suites	SD5	The contract of sales and leases
SB2	Human Rights & Fair Housing	SD7	Forms of Property Ownership
SB3	Land Use & Regulations	TA	Economics
SB4	Law of Agency	TB	Rules & Regulations
SB5	License Law	TD	Transactions & Processes

CONTINUE ▶

TEST DIRECTION

Read the questions carefully and then choose the ONE best answer to each question.

Be sure to allocate your time carefully so you are able to complete the entire test within the testing session. You may go back and review your answers at any time.

You may use any available space in your test booklet for scratch work.

Questions in this booklet are not actual test questions but they are the samples for commonly asked questions.

This test aims to cover all topics which may appear on the actual test. However some topics may not be covered.

Studying this booklet will be preparing you for the actual test. It will not guarantee improving your test score but it will help you pass your exam on the first attempt.

Some useful tips for answering multiple choice questions;

- Start with the questions that you can easily answer.

- Underline the keywords in the question.

- Be sure to read all the choices given.

- Watch for keywords such as NOT, always, only, all, never, completely.

- Do not forget to answer every question.

1

Net operating income or NOI refers to a calculation used to analyze real estate investment generating income.

Which of the following do expenses are deducted from to determine net operating income?

A) Gross income

B) Variable income

C) Vacancy factor

D) Cash flow

2

A **gross lease** is a lease where the tenant pays a flat rental amount, and the landlord pays for all property charges regularly incurred by the ownership.

Which of the following is true about a gross lease?

A) Requires the tenant to pay taxes and insurance

B) Only applies to commercial properties.

C) Vile and repulsive

D) None of the above

3

A sovereign entity exclusively grants a land patent to a particular tract of land.

Which of the following is the use of a land patent?

A) Protect trademark rights to a piece of unique property

B) Fasten two parallel plates at a corner

C) Fasten two different plates at a corner

D) Correct an irregularity in a zoning law

4

When determining a property's value and a budget, which of the following expense accounts for the possibility that the property will not have a paying tenant?

A) Capital expense

B) Replacement allowance

C) Tenancy

D) Vacancy

CONTINUE ▶

5

Which among the following business structures does not require registration with the state?

A) S Corp

B) General Partnership

C) C Corp

D) LLC

6

Which of the following require mortgage brokers to disclose to loan applicants?

A) Amount of credit line

B) Fees

C) Net worth

D) All of the above

7

Market value should exchange on the date of valuation between a willing buyer and a willing seller in an arms-length transaction after proper marketing wherein the parties had each acted knowledgeably, prudently.

Which of the following refers to the factor that exerts the least amount of influence on the value of a seller's property?

A) Local economy

B) The listing agent's opinion

C) Location

D) Supply and demand

8

Closing refers to the last step in making a real estate transaction.

Which of the following is not necessary at a closing?

A) Listing Agent

B) Deed

C) Seller

D) Buyer

9

Which of the following refers to the outside rough surface of a frame structure placed over the studs?

A) Sheathing

B) Paneling

C) Molding

D) Eaves

11

The **arithmetic calculations** refer to the percentage of your income that is taken up by your debt obligations. Lenders look at this percentage to help them decide whether or not you are a credit risk. When you request a mortgage, lenders look for specific defining financial characteristics about you.

Which of the following is used by financial institutions to determine loan amounts for borrowers?

A) Amortization tables

B) Apportionments

C) Quadrennial factors

D) Qualifying ratios

10

Which of the following is required when selling real estate securities?

A) A real estate agent license

B) A Series 7 license

C) Registration with the state

D) All of these answers are correct.

12

Which of the following would the unused prepaid taxes appear on a closing statement?

A) Credit to the seller

B) Credit to the buyer

C) Neither A or B

D) Both A & B

13

Which of the following offers the greatest assurance of title?

A) Warranty deed
B) Sheriff's deed
C) Quitclaim deed
D) Bargain and Sale deed

14

Mortgage brokers help a client to find the best interest rate and terms for a mortgage.

Which of the following register mortgage brokers?

A) Department of Banking
B) Department of Brokerage
C) Department of Mortgage Brokerage
D) Department of State

15

Which of the following would not refer to a transaction where parents are selling to their son and daughter-in-law?

A) Valid
B) Recordable
C) Enforceable
D) An arm's length transaction

16

Deed refers to a legal document which is an official record and proof of ownership of property.

Which of the following is a must for deeds to be recorded?

A) Written
B) Acknowledged
C) Both A & B
D) Neither A or B

17

Which of the following definitions is true for a condo?

A) A special form of condominium ownership

B) A special form of residential and commercial ownership

C) A special form of cooperative and condominium ownership

D) A special form of cooperative ownership

18

Timeshare refers to the arrangement where joint owners have the right to use a property as a vacation home under a time-sharing agreement.

Which of the following types of timeshare does not give you any ownership interest over the property but lets you use the property for a specific period?

A) Licensed timeshare

B) An RTU contract

C) A fixed term timeshare

D) None of the above

19

Appraisal refers to the assessment of real property. Which of the following kinds of appraisal are retail purchasers most likely to rely on?

A) Cost Approach

B) Reconciliation of Value Approach

C) Income Approach

D) Comparative Sales Approach

20

A **clause** in a listing agreement refers to an accord a property owner makes with a real estate broker, saying the owner will pay the broker to lease or sell the property for a given price. An automatic extension makes the listing agreement persist after it expires, for a specified time.

Which of the following is true in the use of automatic extensions of time on listing agreements?

A) A good business practice

B) Illegal

C) Unethical

D) None of the above

21

Which of the following requires the federal government to consider the environmental impact of its projects?

A) CERCLA

B) NEPA

C) NHPA

D) None of the above

22

Which of the following federal laws requires the Good Faith Estimate must be provided to the borrower within three business days after taking a loan application?

A) TILA

B) RESPA

C) HMDA

D) ECOA

23

Which of the following power permits the government to take your private property even if you don't want it to do so?

A) Zoning laws

B) Environmental regulations

C) Eminent domain

D) None, such government action is unconstitutional.

24

If a property is worth $200,000 and an investor expects to be able to earn a net operating income of $15,000 a year, what is the cap rate?

A) 20.5%

B) 15.5%

C) 7.5%

D) 5.5%

25

Which of the following does the IRS use to define a real estate professional?

A) When the taxpayer is a licensed real estate agent or not

B) The number of hours worked in real estate each year

C) The number of real estate properties owned

D) The number of experience years in the real estate industry

26

Your town's zoning laws require an apartment building to provide two and a half parking spaces for every 1,000 square feet of inhabited space.

A local apartment building has 80,000 square feet of apartments. How many parking spaces should it have?

A) 200

B) 180

C) 160

D) 140

27

Which of the following is TRUE regarding desired profit that an investor uses to determine the value of a property?

A) Increasing expenses reach the desired profit.

B) The desired profit is a personal choice for each investor.

C) The desired profit does not affect property valuation.

D) The desired profit is one percent of the purchase price each month.

28

Which of the following types of scam entails homeowners who are encouraged to refinance their property over and over until little or no equity remains?

A) Reverse equity

B) Property skimming

C) Loan flipping

D) Extreme lending

29

Which of the following is true for specific performance as a remedy granted by a court?

A) Requires a party to a contract to pay a specific amount of money damages

B) Requires a party to a contract to renegotiate the contract

C) Requires a party to a contract to perform on the contract

D) Voids the contract

30

A **life estate** refers to the land ownership for a person's lifetime in common and statutory law. However, in legal terms, it is an estate that will terminate at death in which a property can transfer to another person or revert to the original owner.

Which of the following is the interest in a life estate held by a grantor?

A) Primary interest

B) Interest rate

C) Remainder Interest

D) Reversionary interest

31

Installment sale contract refers to the method of sale allowing for partial deferral of capital gain to any future taxation years.

In an installment sale contract on a property, when will the title is conveyed to the purchaser?

A) At the time of the last payment to the seller

B) At the time the contract is signed

C) At the end of the rescission period

D) At the time the full down payment has been turned over to the seller's attorney

32

Which of the following refers to an exclusive agency listing?

A) The agent will have a fee no matter who sells the property whether it's the agent or the seller.

B) Sellers must have the right to use as many brokers as they want. The seller is not obligated to pay any of them if he or she sells the property without the broker's help.

C) Agents only get paid if they sell the property. There is no fee if the owner alone sells the property.

D) All of the above

33

Which of the following is a description of an Article 78 Procedure?

A) Bench warrant for the arrest of a squatter

B) Court order to vacate a condemned property

C) Legal proceeding to appeal a government agency's ruling

D) Law suit to collect damages from a neighbor who encroached on a property line

34

Condominiums are where buyers own the deeds to their dwellings. When you buy into a co-op, you become a shareholder in a corporation that owns the property. As a shareholder, you are entitled to exclusive use of a housing unit in the property.

Which of the following should prospective co-op purchaser have to meet?

A) Board of Directors

B) Broker's attorney

C) Building superintendent

D) City council

CONTINUE ▶

35

When someone (whether a man or a woman) dies having made a valid will, he or she dies "testate". Otherwise, he died "intestate.

A person died "testate", but after an extensive search, there were no additional heirs found.

Which of the following way should the person's real propert transferred by?

A) Devise

B) Demise

C) Escheat to the state

D) Descent and distribution

36

A **condominium** is a type of real estate divided into several units that are each separately owned, surrounded by common areas jointly owned.

Which of the following does condominium purchase involve?

A) Deed transfer

B) Meeting with a Board of Directors

C) Purchase of corporate stock

D) Proprietary Lease

37

A copper mine was considered as the town's biggest employer which recently closed. House values have collapsed, and houses have become difficult to sell at any price.

Which of the following types of consideration is this an example?

A) Economic

B) Government

C) Physical

D) Social

38

Which of the following type of arrangements is useful when companies need to unbind the invested money in an asset for other investments, but the asset still needs to operate?

A) Sale and leaseback

B) Secondary market

C) Joint venture

D) Contingency

67

CONTINUE ▶

39

Which of the following makes the best description of the discounted cash flow method?

A) The total of the future value of rents over a specified period

B) The ratio of rent over the selling price of the home

C) The total of the present value of rents over a specified period

D) A discount paid at the purchase because the seller guarantees cash flow.

40

An **encumbrance** refers to a charge or regulation which is attached to and is binding upon a property. It may affect the clarity of a good title or may diminish the value of a property, but may not prevent the transfer of title.

Which of the following might an encumbrance be?

A) Shared driveway

B) Right of Way

C) Real estate tax lien

D) All of the above

41

Section 1031, a section of the U.S. Internal Revenue Service Code, allows investors to defer capital gains taxes on any exchange of this kind of properties for business or investment purposes.

Which of the following is the term that describes the properties involved in a 1031 exchange?

A) Vacant properties

B) Transitional properties

C) Community-owned properties

D) Like-kind properties

42

Which of the following is the general power of government to enact laws and regulations that limit personal conduct and property rights for the protection of the health, safety, and welfare of the general public?

A) Common law

B) Enumerated powers

C) Police power

D) None of the answers are correct.

43

A buyer purchases a home for $4,500,000. They have acquired a 30-year loan at 6.5% interest with a 20% downpayment.

Which of the following is the amount of interest that the buyer needs to pay over the life of the loan?

A) $4,591,601.60

B) $4,321,125.30

C) $4,186,475.50

D) $2,134,925.10

44

Dave wants to buy a real estate investment which he can expect an 8% cap rate.

If the net operating income from a specific property is $6500 per year, what is the value to Dave of the home using the direct capitalization method?

A) $52,000

B) $78,000

C) $81,250

D) $84,500

45

Jones v. Alfred H. Mayer Co. could regulate the sale of private property to prevent racial discrimination.

Which of the following provisions does the Jones v. Mayer Decision uphold?

A) Article 12A

B) Civil Rights Act of 1866

C) Federal Fair Housing Act of 1968

D) New York State Executive Law

46

A property originally purchased a year ago for $1,750,000 is now valued at $2,080,000. What is the percentage rate of appreciation?

Note: round to the nearest tenth by rounding up five and above and rounding down four and below.

A) 84.0%

B) 18.9%

C) 17.5%

D) 8.4%

47

A **prudent investment** is to use financial assets that are suitable for the risk and return profile and the time horizon of a given investor.

Which of the following would not be a prudent investment for a first-time investor?

A) Six-family residential building

B) Vacant land

C) Thirty-unit suburban motel

D) Five-unit strip shopping center

48

Drew bought a rental property for $151,000. He only now just found out about the concept of a cap rate. The property has revenue of $18,000 a year and net operating expenses of $4,000 each year.

Which of the following is the cap rate of this property?

A) 11.92%

B) 9.27%

C) 6.27%

D) 2.65%

SECTION 5

#	Answer	Topic	Subtopic	#	Answer	Topic	Subtopic	#	Answer	Topic	Subtopic	#	Answer	Topic	Subtopic
1	A	TA	SA1	13	A	TD	SD2	25	B	TD	SD4	37	A	TA	SA7
2	D	TD	SD5	14	A	TA	SA4	26	A	TD	SD1	38	A	TA	SA1
3	B	TD	SD2	15	D	TD	SD2	27	B	TA	SA3	39	C	TA	SA3
4	D	TA	SA3	16	C	TD	SD2	28	C	TA	SA4	40	D	TA	SA2
5	B	TD	SD4	17	C	TB	SB1	29	C	TD	SD5	41	D	TD	SD2
6	B	TA	SA4	18	B	TD	SD7	30	D	TA	SA2	42	C	TB	SB3
7	B	TD	SD6	19	D	TA	SA1	31	D	TD	SD5	43	A	TA	SA2
8	A	TD	SD2	20	B	TA	SA7	32	C	TD	SD5	44	C	TA	SA3
9	A	TD	SD1	21	C	TB	SB3	33	C	TB	SB3	45	B	TB	SB2
10	B	TD	SD4	22	B	TA	SA4	34	A	TB	SB1	46	B	TA	SA1
11	D	TA	SA6	23	C	TD	SD7	35	C	TB	SB4	47	B	TA	SA1
12	A	TD	SD2	24	C	TD	SD4	36	A	TB	SB1	48	B	TA	SA3

Topics & Subtopics

Code	Description	Code	Description
SA1	Commercial Investment	SD1	Construction & Environmental Issues
SA2	Estates & Interests	SD2	Deeds & Title Closing Costs
SA3	Income Approach to Real Estate Valuation	SD4	Real Estate Investment & Analysis
SA4	Mortgage Brokerage	SD5	The contract of sales and leases
SA6	Real Estate Math	SD6	Valuation
SA7	Real Estate Market	SD7	Forms of Property Ownership
SB1	Condominiums & Suites	TA	Economics
SB2	Human Rights & Fair Housing	TB	Rules & Regulations
SB3	Land Use & Regulations	TD	Transactions & Processes
SB4	Law of Agency		

CONTINUE ▶

TEST DIRECTION

DIRECTIONS

Read the questions carefully and then choose the ONE best answer to each question.

Be sure to allocate your time carefully so you are able to complete the entire test within the testing session. You may go back and review your answers at any time.

You may use any available space in your test booklet for scratch work.

Questions in this booklet are not actual test questions but they are the samples for commonly asked questions.

This test aims to cover all topics which may appear on the actual test. However some topics may not be covered.

Studying this booklet will be preparing you for the actual test. It will not guarantee improving your test score but it will help you pass your exam on the first attempt.

Some useful tips for answering multiple choice questions;

- Start with the questions that you can easily answer.

- Underline the keywords in the question.

- Be sure to read all the choices given.

- Watch for keywords such as NOT, always, only, all, never, completely.

- Do not forget to answer every question.

CONTINUE ▶

1

When a homeowner has a contract with an agent in selling a home, the listing agreement has a set expiration date.

Which of the following refer to the most common reason for listings expiring?

A) The property was priced too high.
B) The property was in poor condition.
C) The property was not in a good location.
D) The property did not get adequate exposure to the market.

2

Which of the following does a real estate agent be guilty of if he suggests to a client that he moves into an area where he will "fit into"?

A) Steering
B) Redlining
C) Flipping
D) Blockbusting

3

Functional obsolescence refers to a reduction of an object's usefulness or desirability because of an outdated design feature that cannot be easily changed.

Which of the following would be the most likely example of functional obsolescence?

A) An entirely pink tile bathroom floor with matching countertop and a shower surround
B) A change in zoning is permitting mixed use in what used to be just a residential zone.
C) The building of a stadium across the highway
D) The presence of nearby Section 8 housing

4

An **automatic renewal clause** also called as self-renewal or evergreen clause acts to renew a contract if notice to terminate perpetually is not provided within a generally specific and relatively small window of time (for example, 30 days before the end of the term).

Which of the following refers to an automatic renewal clause in a lease?

A) Illegal
B) Good for the landlord and tenant
C) Good for the tenant
D) Good for the landlord

5

Source of income describes where the money comes from. For an individual income could be from multiple sources such as employment, investment, and welfare for example. For business, it could be from a particular market, products, customers, investments or government grants.

Which of the following is a source of income other than rent?

A) Laundromats

B) Mortgage interest

C) Property taxes

D) Vacancy

6

Which of the following is determined by a real estate agent when gathering data for a seller?

A) A reasonable asking price for the property on the market

B) The value a lender will place on the property when it is purchased.

C) The exact value of the property on that particular date

D) None of the above

7

Restriction is an official rule whichlimits what you can do or amount or size of something.

Which of the following estates has the fewest restrictions on the holder of it?

A) Absolute life estate

B) Fee simple determinable

C) Fee simple absolute

D) Legal title

8

Which of the following is the phenomenon of owing more at the end of the year than at the beginning?

A) Deficiency

B) Negative amortization

C) Wrap around mortgage

D) Usury

9

Lally Column is a tubular steel column filled with concrete and used as a supporting member in a building.

Where do they are normally found?

A) Attic

B) Basement

C) Bathrooms

D) Closets

10

Which of the following is the maximum age for a real estate salesperson/broker?

A) 20

B) 24

C) 65

D) None of the above

11

Which of the following is termed for a legal description written regarding angles and distances is known?

A) Plat of Lots

B) Lot and Block

C) Metes and Bounds

D) None of the above

12

Milly woke up one morning after a violent storm and discovered that a large chunk of her riverbank is gone.

Which of the following does this situation fall?

A) Attrition

B) Dissipation

C) Reliction

D) None of the answers are correct.

13

A **short sale** is where the net proceeds from selling the property will fall short of the debts secured by liens against the property.

Which of the following refers to the outstanding balance owed on a loan after the property has been sold at a short sale?

A) Arrears
B) Deficit
C) Deficiency
D) None of the answers are correct.

14

Which of the following describes alienation?

A) Transferring real property from one person to another
B) The legal process involved in obtaining an easement by prescription
C) Acquiring property in an open, hostile, and continuous manner over time
D) Acquiring alluvion through a court proceeding

15

British Thermal Unit (BTU) is part of the British Imperial system of units, its counterpart in the metric system.

Which of the following does the British Thermal Unit measure?

A) Skill
B) Energy
C) Electricity
D) None of the above

16

Termite is an insect living in large colonies with different castes, typically in a mound of cemented earth.

Which of the following may stop termites?

A) DDT
B) PCBs
C) Chlordane
D) None of the above

17

Which of the following describes a tenancy by the entirety?

A) Equal or unequal undivided ownership between two or more people

B) Ownership that's available for Limited Liabilities

C) Ownership which requires the four unities: Interest, Possession, Time, and Title

D) Ownership that is available only to married couples, tenancy by the entirety means that property may not be sold without the agreement of both parties.

18

Building foundation supports a building from underneath.

Which of the following is the material most commonly used for foundations?

A) Concrete

B) Copper

C) PVC

D) Wood

19

Which of the following refers to an appraisal process that uses comparisons of similar properties in the same neighborhood?

A) Cost Approach

B) Pricing Method

C) Market Data Approach

D) All of the above

20

Which of the following describes a legal method of minimizing or decreasing an investor's taxable income and, therefore, his or her tax liability?

A) Insurance claim

B) Return on investment

C) Tax shelter

D) Vacancy loss

21

Marty and Belle hold a piece of property as joint tenants. Marty decides to sell his interest to Clint.

How do Belle and Clint hold their interest?

A) There are insufficient facts to make this determination.
B) Tenants in common
C) Tenants by the entirety
D) Joint and several tenants

22

"Time is of the Essence" is used as a phrase in a contract referring to the performance by a party at or within the period specified in the contract. Failure to perform within the required time constitutes a breach in the contract.

Which of the following happens to the closing date when "time is of the essence is invoked?

A) Is dropped from the contract
B) Loses its importance
C) Becomes significant
D) None of the above

23

A **septic tank** refers to a watertight chamber which is usually made of concrete, fiberglass or PVC through which domestic wastewater flows for primary treatment.

Which of the following is the percentage of American homes having septic systems?

A) 25%
B) 15%
C) 10%
D) 5%

24

Which of the following does the remaining fuel in a storage tank at closing is being apportioned and paid?

A) Current market value
B) The average price of advertised prices at the time the seller purchased it
C) The price at which the seller purchased the fuel
D) None of the above

78

CONTINUE ▶

25

Ownership of mineral rights refers to an estate in real property which is the right of the owner to exploit, mine, or produce any or all of the minerals lying below the surface of the property.

Which of the following may an owner of both a surface and mineral estate not do with them?

A) Sell the mineral rights.

B) Lease the mineral rights.

C) Sell the surface estate but keep the mineral rights.

D) None of the answers are correct.

26

Lead refers to a naturally occurring element which is found in small amounts in the earth's crust.

When did federal lead-based paint disclosure laws go into effect?

A) 1995

B) 1977

C) 1996

D) 1994

27

Undivided loyalty prohibits an agent from getting any advance interests adverse to his/her client or conducting his/her client's business to benefit him/herself or others.

Which of the following is considered in undivided loyalty?

A) Agent

B) Broker

C) Client

D) Customer

28

Anne has a future interest in a house, but she only is entitled to possession of the house if Don stops using it as a residence.

What type of future interest does Anne have?

A) Her interest is vested.

B) Her interest is contingent.

C) She doesn't have a future interest.

D) She has a future possessory interest.

CONTINUE ▶

29

Comparables refers to a real estate appraisal term referring to properties with characteristics that are similar to a subject property whose value is being sought.

What is the minimum number of comps required by most secondary lenders to ensure an accurate estimate of value when performing the sales comparison approach?

A) 5

B) 4

C) 3

D) 2

30

You are trying to price a property. Five years ago, it was sold for $1,450,000, but property values in this particular neighborhood have decreased by an average of 5 percent since then.

Which of the following is the rough value of this property?

A) $1,400,000

B) $1,377,500

C) $1,300,000

D) $825,000

31

Obtaining a **mortgage** is a crucial part in the buying process and securing mortgage pre-qualification, and pre-approval are necessary steps to assure lenders that you'll be able to afford payments.

Which of the following may pre-approval letter be substituted?

A) State disclosure form

B) Mortgage commitment

C) Lead-based paint disclosure

D) Agent qualifying

32

Two almost identical houses are located in an A+ rated school district and a mediocre school district, respectively. Because of this, the house in the A+ school district is likely to sell for more money.

Which of the following types of consideration does this indicate?

A) Economic

B) Government

C) Physical

D) Social

33

A **contract clause** refers to a specific section within a written contract that define the duties, rights, and privileges that each party has under the contract terms

Which of the following describes a contract clause that will allow either party to void the contract if a certain condition occurs?

A) Cogency
B) Contingency
C) Deficiency
D) Disciple

34

Which of the following refers to the process where there is an increase in real property by nature such as the buildup of silt?

A) Accretion
B) Addition
C) Erosion
D) Probate

35

Which of the following would a $400/month tenant's prepaid rent appear on a closing statement dated April 15th?

A) Debit buyer $200
B) Debit seller $200
C) Debit buyer $200, Credit seller $200
D) Debit seller $200, Credit buyer $200

36

The **trustee** manages or holds assets, cash or a property title. Which of the following benefits when the trustee held in a property?

A) Beneficiary
B) Grantor
C) Heir
D) Decedent

37

A broker received a commission of $180,975 for having sold a property priced at $3,450,000.

Which of the following was the broker's commission rate?

A) 5.0%
B) 5.5%
C) 6.0%
D) 6.5%

38

The **cost approach** refers to a real estate valuation method that surmises that the price a buyer should pay for a piece of property should equal the cost to build an equivalent building.

Which of the following circumstances would a cost approach be most useful?

A) A retail buyer who is looking for a home they plan to stay in for many years
B) An investor who wants to maximize his profit margin from renting out a property
C) A new construction property in an area with nearby available land
D) All of these answers are equally appropriate.

39

James is deeding his mortgage-free house to his niece. Is his deed required to show good consideration to be valid in this case?

A) No, because family transfers are an exemption from the law.
B) No, because no lien holder involved and there is no mortgage in the house.
C) Yes, unless she is deeding it to him in her will.
D) Yes, because all deeds must show proper consideration to be valid.

40

A **title** refers to proof of ownership on a property.

Which of the following offers the least assurance of title?

A) Trust deed
B) Full Warranty Deed
C) Bargain and Sale deed with covenants
D) Bargain and Sale deed without covenants

41

Peter wants to sell his three-bedroom Tudor house for $250,000, but all other similar homes in the area are selling for $225,000 each.

Which of the following principles tells that Peter's home is more likely to be worth $225,000?

A) Contribution
B) Balance
C) Substitution
D) Supply

42

Mortgage refers to a loan which is secured by property or real estate. In exchange for funds received by the homebuyer to buy property or a home, a lender gets the promise of that buyer to pay back the funds within a specific time frame for a particular cost.

Which of the following make home mortgages available to the public?

A) Credit unions
B) Mortgage bankers
C) Savings banks
D) All of the above

43

Which of the following refers to the general term in real estate that means a person legally owns a piece of real estate and has the right to use and enjoy it?

A) Title
B) Legal title
C) Equitable title
D) All of the answers are correct

44

Urea-formaldehyde foam insulation (UFFI) was used extensively in the 1970s. Homeowners used UFFI as a wall cavity filler at the time to conserve energy. Then, it was injected inside the walls, the curing process occurs, and the final product acts as an insulating agent.

Which of the following is the advantage of urea formaldehyde foam insulation over other insulation?

A) Less expensive
B) Contaminant-free
C) Easy to install
D) None of the above

45

The U.S. government describes **lead-based paint** as a paint or coating containing lead in 0.5% by weight or equal to or greater than one milligram per square centimeter.

Which of the following statements is not true?

A) The presence of lead paint in homes must only be disclosed if the home is being purchased using an FHA loan.
B) The presence of lead paint in homes must never be disclosed if the home is being purchased using an FHA loan.
C) Private information must need consent from the homeowners.
D) Neither of the above

46

Section 1031 is under the section of the U.S. Internal Revenue Service Code tackling any exchange of properties for business or investment purposes.

Which of the following is the primary purpose of a 1031 exchange?

A) Transfer owned property to a family member before the owner's death without paying taxes.

B) Transfer the property to a non-family member upon the owner's death.

C) Delay paying taxes when selling one rental investment and using the funds to purchase a similar income producing property.

D) None of these answers are correct.

47

Multifamily residential refers to a type of housing where several separate residential units are within one building or several buildings within one complex.

Which of the following is a disadvantage of owning a multi-family housing?

A) Owners may receive multiple rent checks each month.

B) A vacancy in one unit would not eliminate income flow from the property.

C) The owner may be able to avoid commercial financing if he or she lives in one of the units.

D) Generally, there are less potential buyers for units in multi-family properties.

48

Which of the following refers to the situation called Pro-ration during a corporate action in which the available cash or shares are not sufficient to satisfy the offers tendered by shareholders?

A) The process of settling a will

B) The process of a government taking an individual's land under eminent domain

C) The time necessary for a variance to hold before the planning board

D) The apportionment of expenses and assets of buyer and seller at closing

SECTION 6

#	Answer	Topic	Subtopic	#	Answer	Topic	Subtopic	#	Answer	Topic	Subtopic	#	Answer	Topic	Subtopic
1	A	TD	SD5	13	C	TD	SD7	25	D	TD	SD7	37	B	TA	SA6
2	A	TD	SD4	14	A	TD	SD2	26	C	TD	SD1	38	C	TA	SA7
3	A	TA	SA7	15	B	TD	SD1	27	C	TA	SA1	39	C	TD	SD2
4	A	TD	SD5	16	D	TD	SD1	28	B	TD	SD7	40	D	TD	SD2
5	A	TA	SA3	17	D	TD	SD2	29	C	TA	SA4	41	C	TA	SA7
6	A	TD	SD4	18	A	TD	SD1	30	B	TA	SA2	42	D	TA	SA5
7	C	TD	SD7	19	C	TD	SD6	31	D	TA	SA5	43	A	TD	SD7
8	B	TA	SA5	20	C	TA	SA6	32	D	TA	SA7	44	D	TD	SD1
9	B	TD	SD1	21	B	TD	SD7	33	B	TD	SD5	45	A	TD	SD1
10	D	TA	SA7	22	C	TD	SD5	34	A	TD	SD2	46	C	TD	SD4
11	C	TD	SD2	23	A	TD	SD1	35	D	TD	SD2	47	D	TD	SD4
12	D	TD	SD7	24	A	TD	SD2	36	A	TA	SA2	48	D	TD	SD2

Topics & Subtopics

Code	Description	Code	Description
SA1	Commercial Investment	SD2	Deeds & Title Closing Costs
SA2	Estates & Interests	SD4	Real Estate Investment & Analysis
SA3	Income Approach to Real Estate Valuation	SD5	The contract of sales and leases
SA4	Mortgage Brokerage	SD6	Valuation
SA5	Real Estate Finance	SD7	Forms of Property Ownership
SA6	Real Estate Math	TA	Economics
SA7	Real Estate Market	TD	Transactions & Processes
SD1	Construction & Environmental Issues		

CONTINUE ▶

34162866R00054

Made in the USA
Middletown, DE
23 January 2019